Ridiculously Old
and
Getting Better:

Ageless Lessons from a
Very Old Stand-Up Comedian

Lynn Ruth Miller

RIDICULOUSLY OLD AND GETTIING BETTER:
Ageless Lessons from a Very Old Stand-Up Comedian

By Lynn Ruth Miller

Eldership
Academy Press
www.eldershipacademypress.org

Second Edition, 2021

©2021 Eldership Academy Press.

Published by Eldership Academy Press
March 2021, San Francisco, California

Paperback Second Edition ISBN: 978-0-98470-979-3
eBook First Edition ISBN: 978-0-64511-171-2

1. Comedy | 2. Aging | 3. Gerontology
4. Stand Up | 5. Philosophy | 6. Psychology

Printed and distributed worldwide by IngramSpark

FOREWORD

At sixty-three I am caught in the middle of a busy life. I am smitten by Lynn, her freedom to move any which way she is called: Pacifica, San Francisco, London, Berlin, Dortmund, Brighton, Paris. A few years ago she lost her house in foreclosure. She had lived in it for some twenty-eight years. A few years earlier, she had broken her heel. Living on a hill in Pacifica, she had a difficult time getting around. Her neighbors were not around to help—either they were busy or they just ignored her. I told her that she did not want to be living in such a neighborhood, so it was good that she lost the house. The universe takes care of our attachments.

It's a common belief that older adults are always tired, ornery and unhappy. Movies, TV commercials and late night punch lines all assume older adults are hapless buffoons with nothing better to do than yell "Get off of my lawn!" They also prefer to complain endlessly about their physical ailments to anyone who will listen.

This is largely a myth. While physical and cognitive decline are a natural part of the aging process, the truth of aging is very different than popular culture would have us believe.

Humans are actually the happiest at the early and late times of their lives. Stanford's Laura Carstensen calls it The Happiness Curve — or the U-Curve of Happiness — and she's spent over three decades researching the topic. Head of the Stanford Center on Longevity, Carstensen's research on happiness found that older adults were actually happier overall than at any other time in their life since childhood. They are happier than their teenage years, their twenties and thirties, happier even than when they became wealthy and successful.

Carstensen says there is one key to her findings: time. When humans realize that they have less time left, they savor life more. They shift their perspective and spend more emotional energy on what matters.

In his forties, author of *The Happiness Curve* Jonathan Rauch had noticed both in himself and his middle-aged friends a steadily rising dissatisfaction with their existence. It didn't seem to correlate with the external world since he and his friends were all successful by society's standards, with good jobs and plenty of money. It wasn't depression or anxiety, but more accurately a confusing malaise, an almost existential ennui, something he termed "an accumulated drizzle of disappointment." Drip, drip, drip.

What Rauch had discovered was precisely what wisdom traditions have known for centuries, even millennia. True happiness doesn't spring from wealth or success. It arises spontaneously when we learn to value compassion and connection over competition and achievement.

The great 13th century Persian love poet Rumi wrote that the fruit that's the ripest hangs the lowest — a nod to the aging process. Chinese sages tell us the bamboo that stands the tallest also bows the deepest. The German philosopher Goethe said that the highest achievement in life means deepening both our personalities and our understanding of the world. Lynn Ruth Miller tells us to live our lives at any age.

Nader R. Shabahangi
CO-DIRECTOR, ELDERSHIP ACADEMY PRESS

BERLIN

Looking back on 86 years...
What I have learned.

Old age and the passage of time teach all things.
SOPHOCLES

We all wish we knew what life has taught us when we were younger. We would have made wiser decisions. We would not have worried so much about who we were and what we would become. When I think of the uncertainties and the fears I grappled with when I was young and the terror I felt at the prospect of not being able to take care of myself now that I am in my eighties, I realize that most of those worries were meaningless. And that is why I have written this book.

It occurred to me that if I could share some of the lessons I have learned from living this life with people younger than I, perhaps I could save them from the stress and worry that I suffered as I traveled through the years.

But what exactly has my life been? I was born in 1933 in a very different world than the one we live in today. My life was peppered with false starts, near misses and failures, but somehow I managed to become a new person every few years. I have been with varying degrees of success a student, a wife, an elementary school teacher, a telephone Madame, a TV producer, a watchman, an art teacher, a professor, a journalist, a secretary, a novelist, a storyteller and a reviewer when at seventy years of age, I discovered stand–up comedy. That career graduated into burlesque and cabaret. It took me across the ocean to London and it is what I do today.

All those vocations and all those adventures taught me a lot about living. I figured out what kind of person I wanted to be, and I learned to accept the kind of person I became. I learned that I alone am responsible for my happiness and that the art of living a full and rich life is to recognize opportunity when it comes my way. I learned that all fear is counterproductive and that hope fuels success. I figured out that no dream is impossible if you put the necessary work into it to make it happen. I discovered that the only way to have a successful relationship with another is to forge a solid one with yourself. I realized that I am not perfect and that I do not want to be. Perfection is boring. It is our flaws that make us interesting to others and most important, to ourselves.

I wish I had known all this when I was struggling to cope with an unhappy childhood, two disastrous marriages, career obstacles and all the glass ceilings society builds so that who we are and what the world tells us we should be cannot ever match.

I realize now how useless fear and doubt are and how they block us from finding our true path. I want to share all this understanding that took me eighty-five years or more to figure out. I am hoping it will save you from a few false steps and erase a lot of unnecessary uncertainties. I love being old. I love it because I am not afraid of anything anymore. Nothing

Ridiculously Old and Getting Better

is going to happen to me that I haven't faced and conquered before. In this book, I will give you my observations on what life has taught me. I am hoping these stories will give you new insights and encourage you to grab life by the tail and run with it.

That is what I do.

> Change your thoughts and you change your world.
> NORMAN VINCENT PEALE

Can't Wait to Be Old!

> Aging is an extraordinary process
> where you become the person you
> always should have been.
> DAVID BOWIE

The ancient Greeks had a saying that if the gods really wanted to punish you, they would make sure that your first forty years of life were filled with ease and success. This seems a strange concept, as today we try hard to give our children a so-called happy childhood, to protect them from harm and unnecessary difficulties. A good life is synonymous with the absence of suffering and pain, a lack of hardship and adversity. What were these Greeks thinking? Very simply that if we humans did not confront misfortune in our early years, we would be woefully unprepared to face the depth, complexities, and richness of our later years. Imagine for a moment that only in your forties would you begin to understand that life does not always go exactly the way you want it to, does not always flow smoothly and effortlessly. You would be in for a very rude and painful awakening. It's in our early years that we learn about the give-and-take of life, the compromises we must make, the struggles we must undergo to become a member of our human community. These are the years when we try to form an identity, when we are anxious to see if we can take our seat among our peers and be successful in their eyes. Establishing ourselves is often an arduous process, but it prepares us for possibly more difficult chapters in our later years, including our elder years.

What does being elderly mean, anyway? Aren't elders all different? Aren't we each the product of our own unique experience—the rejections we have faced, the walls we have had to climb, the conditions imposed on us that we couldn't help? Yet if, in our long lives, we have each taken responsibility for what we become, if we have insisted on fashioning ourselves into someone we love and respect, then perhaps we can share that wisdom as elders.

GLASGOW

CHAPTER 1

Am I the Person I Was Meant to Be?

As soon as you feel too old to do a thing, do it.

MARGARET DELAND

How much of what we do and how we live is determined by what we are told will make us happy? When we were children our parents and teachers gave us the guidelines that structured our lives. We watched how our parents lived and we either thought, "Why can't I be like that," or, "I will never live an empty, materialistic life like that!"

The result is that we waste a lot of energy emulating our family's lifestyle, or rebelling against it. That didn't leave us much to discover on our own unique path in childhood. If you are busy trying to be just like your mother so your daddy will love you, there isn't very much time left to figure out what kind of person you really want to be. If you spend your time trying to be "one of the guys" because your father loves macho sports and goes bowling with his gang, you never have much time to explore the unique sensitivities you have that might take you in a new and exciting direction.

As we got older, the demands of our education molded our activities and our goals. We were absorbed in preparing for a vocation that would give our life the meaning we thought it needed. We devoted our time trying to learn life lessons from books. We emulated the people we admired, because they seemed glamorous or exciting to us. Our teens and twenties were years filled with imitation instead of original thought.

By the time we got to our thirties, our job and family determined what we did and how we structured our life. We were beginning to earn enough money to pay the rent, buy the food, and support the family. Sadly, there was very little energy left to explore a hobby or wander into a new way of living that might satisfy our soul.

Suddenly, we are fifty years old doing the same job, living the same routine that we have been doing for far too many years, and wondering why we are bored and dissatisfied. We ask, "Is this the person I was meant to be?" This is the time in life when women begin to doubt their value because they are approaching menopause, the children have left home, and sex with their partner holds few surprises. Men look at their career and realize they will never climb the ladder to the success they thought they would find. Many of them are weighed down with responsibilities that have become burdens to them.

And that should be a turning point for us all. It takes courage to break out of this malaise. But I promise it will make all the difference. I was forty-eight years old when I decided, "The hell with convention; the hell with trying to work for someone else." I had moved to Oklahoma City and wrote for three publications with weekly and daily deadlines, for substandard wages. Finally, I said to myself: "I must have more out of life. I am not doing one single thing for myself, and the job I have is not paying me enough to endure this kind of dissatisfaction."

I decided to sell everything I had and travel through u.
western United States to discover whatever there was to disc
I still remember my mother's dismay. "Nice Jewish girls do not
do that," she said. But at that point I was tired of being a nice
Jewish girl. I wanted to build a life.

It takes a lot of backbone to break out of the accepted patterns
of life you have accepted as the "right way." Yet, at some point,
all of us need to take that leap of faith in our own judgment. We
need to do this to fulfill the most important task we have: living
the only life we have. People are living so much longer than in
previous generations. If we're fortunate, we have many more
years ahead of us than our parents and grandparents had. By the
time we are in our sixties, we have established our place in our
community. By then, we can find out who that person is who has
been inside us, trying desperately to emerge.

But how do you know who that person really is? How do you figure out what you really want out of life when you have spent fifty
or sixty years doing what you "should" do—and what you must
do to survive in a society that values surface accomplishments
and material gain above exploration of the soul?

Each of us must answer that question in his or her own way. An
eighty-year old man from England suffered unbearable back
and muscle pain. He loathed doctors and detested medicine.
Yet, he was determined to live his remaining years free of pain.
His solution was one which no one would ever dream could
work. He had always loved dance, and his special love was
ballet. So it was at eighty that he began taking lessons, first in

BEIJING

a group and then privately, to learn the fundamentals of ballet. His family was convinced he would only make his aches and pains worse. That his mobility, already limited, would soon cease. They were wrong. The more this gentleman used muscles he had neglected for so many years, the more they adapted to the demands he made on them. He danced. He leapt and twirled, he swayed and stepped to beautiful music. Now, at ninety, he dances on stage with major companies.

Impossible? Only to those who are afraid to try something new. Ridiculous? Only to those who do not realize that it's the *trying* that matters, the journey that fulfills us. The destination means nothing—because once we get there, we are done. I met a woman in London who was long retired and seemed content to support her daughter's dance career and care for her grandchildren. She smiled when I described my many activities and she said, "I lead a very quiet life."

"Do you like it?" I asked.

"Yes, I do. And on Tuesdays, I sing for Alzheimer's patients."

That is a beautiful thing she is doing. It may not seem exciting to her, but although she doesn't know it, she found her new calling. If you want your life to wind down so you can give yourself the opportunity to savor the flowers and notice the small, sweet moments, that is all to the good. But if you find yourself unhappily living the same day over and over again, then you have forgotten the most important opportunity all of us have: to expand our personal universe and to use all the lessons we learned yesterday to make a better tomorrow.

DUBLIN

We are not alone in our world. The beauty of life is connecting with others. As we grow older, we need to expand our circle of friends to include every age. Life is like a stew: the more types of people you interact with and the more you reach out to others, the richer it tastes. My lovely friend Laura had spent most of her life writing for newspapers in Scotland, and snorting cocaine. Then she took a trip to Kenya and got to know people who had less materially than her, yet, they supported one another; they enjoyed each other's company. In Laura's eyes, they radiated a happiness she seldom experienced.

Laura goes to Kenya several times a year now to teach health and nutrition. She encourages her students to expand their creative projects and she takes the results home to sell in her London shop, paying them London prices! She is using the money she once used for her drug habit to finance her new passion. It took her well into her fifties to find that passion and discover that she had the courage to pursue it.

Points to Think About:

What kind of world do I want to live in?

How do I find my voice in this world?

How do I speak about the challenges and problems I see in the world?

What responsibility will I assume for this world?

BONN

CHAPTER 2

Find the Spark and Fan Your Passion

We must act out a passion before we
can feel it.

JEAN-PAUL SARTRE

How do you know what you want, what wants to live inside of you? What inner reality wants to come alive? For most of our lives, our family and our peers tell us what we should want from life and what constitutes the good life. When we arrive at middle age, we have been so busy achieving goals others have defined for us that we have never taken the opportunity to explore our own psyche. We have no idea what we really want to do with the rest of our life. We do not have a passion because we have never had the time to consider all the options open to us.

How do you fan that inner spark that is smoldering within you? How do you discover ways to nurture your passion and bring it to life? I was talking to a group of middle-aged women in Dublin about following one's dream, when one woman spoke up. "I have worked all my life and just retired. I have no idea what I want to do now." Who can blame her? We spend so much of the first half of our life establishing a base for ourselves—earning money, building a home, raising a family, creating a career—that we have no time to daydream about that certain something that would feed our soul. We have been too busy feeding our body.

When we were children, we had time to let our mind wander into unknown territory. Our imagination explored the heights of the universe, the depths of the earth, and the breadth of human experience. We dared to wonder what it would be like to explore China, fly to the moon, or catch that star shining through our window. As we grew older, we had no time for those foolish dreams and impossible goals. We were building the image of ourselves that we would show to others, one that would make us acceptable to the rest of society. That is a task that takes all our energy; nothing is left for whimsy and fanciful meanderings. Living the first part of our adult life leaves little time to wonder what it would be like to dig for gold or soar to the moon.

Perhaps the first step to discovering your passion is to let your mind wander. Sit in a rocking chair and do nothing at all. How contrary that is to our modern, fast-paced culture! Finding your passion is like finding the love of your life. You cannot rush it or plan it; you need to stumble on it while on your way to somewhere else. You need the courage to depart from the known and explore an unknown that fascinates you for no apparent reason. You need to tune in to your unconscious dreams—and allow yourself to be surprised at how real they can become.

The reason so few of us grab for the gold ring that glitters in our imagination is that we are afraid we will be judged. We are petrified that we will fail in front of someone else. We all play the "what if" card: What if I make a fool of myself? What if I can't do it? What if I waste all that time and energy and never achieve the goal?

The first step to discovering nirvana is to realize that there is no such thing as failure. Everything you do becomes a part of you, a building block that forms who you are. When I was a teenager, I wanted to attend Stanford University more than anything in the world, but I was afraid to apply. I didn't think I could bear that inevitable letter of refusal. I didn't think I could face my parents who thought so little of me and hear their "I told you so." I would be humiliated, and I didn't think I could bear that. Instead, I applied to universities that I thought would give me a better shot at success, ones that were not so selective, that didn't do a great deal of weeding out after they admitted hopeful seventeen-year-olds embarking on their initial journey into higher education. I filled out applications to five schools, but the one I wanted most (after Stanford) was the University of Michigan, and sure enough, I was accepted. It wasn't the school for me, but it was a very fine university.

Being in college opened my eyes to the world of drama and classical music. It showed me the value of creativity and the intense pleasure that is possible from appreciating a work of art. The university was my first step toward the life I live now, immersed in entertainment and the arts. I didn't know that then. All I knew was that I had to prepare to earn a living and develop in a profession that made sense to me. I chose education and became a teacher.

That was my beginning—but it was not my passion. When I was thirty years old, now twice divorced, battling an eating disorder, and defeated in every facet of the life I was trying to forge for myself, I gathered the courage to apply to the university I had always wanted to attend: Stanford. I instinctively knew this was the place that would open up my potential, and I was right. I sent in my application, resigned to experience yet another setback, another failure, another rejection. I had nothing to lose anymore. I could not possibly be humiliated more than I had been for the past ten years. I was too numbed by a series of misjudgments and dismal realities that defined my life up until that moment.

When I was accepted at Stanford, it was the "yes" that turned a major tide for me. At Stanford I discovered one of my fundamental talents: I could write. I had a way with words and loved playing with them to paint a picture in someone else's mind. I unearthed an ability I should have recognized in childhood but I was too busy creating a life defined by my parents and my peers to notice it. In fact, I began writing poetry when I was six. Through the years, I scribbled on the backs of envelopes and in the margins of school notebooks. Sometimes I would gather enough courage to send them into a contest or the school paper, and many of my attempts to say something others would want to read were published. In time, I was writing for my high school newspaper on a regular basis, but I never considered my compositions anything but recreation. Writing a poem about a lamppost wouldn't earn a living. Creating a saga about the future wouldn't find me the husband I was supposed to capture before I was twenty-one.

At Stanford I unearthed a talent, but I still had not found my passion. That took many more years filled with false starts and adventures. These led me down many paths, but not the one that would feed my heart and soul. My friend George went to community college where he majored in parks and recreation. This was the vocation that would get him a job with the city and give him the security and fringe benefits his parents never had. He had

TOKYO

been working as a recreation leader for many years when one day he had an idea that would send him on the road to his real life's work. George had always loved theater and he noted that most adult activities were centered on crafts and sports. Why couldn't he set up a program for others like himself who loved to act but had no aspirations of actually taking the time or doing the training to go on stage?

It took some fast-talking and a lot of convincing, but eventually he was able to establish a free theater using members of the local community. As the years progressed, he became adept at directing plays, producing them with proper publicity and scenic design. He staged classics as well as modern and *avant-garde* plays, giving members of his community a creative, dramatic outlet and the deep satisfaction that can come with performance. He also sharpened their ability to appreciate and understand the professional theater they paid to see. Purely by accident, George found a passion which is still with him today. It wasn't the road he intended to travel at all, but it is the one he travels now.

Mary trained as a nurse and pursued that profession for sixteen years. During that time she was plagued with severe depression, anxiety attacks, and the feeling that she was racing as fast as she could without going anywhere. She married, she switched specialties, and yet she could not shake the feeling that she was always in the wrong place at the wrong time. Finally, she became so tense and anxious that she was forced to take a leave of absence from her job.

Away from work, she spent time going to psychiatrists and counselors. She took a great deal of medication and none of it helped.

She felt that she was losing herself and would never figure out who she really was. She took long, aimless walks, slept a lot, and was miserable. Then one day a friend asked her if she would dog-sit her poodle. Mary brought the dog home, and while she was taking it out for a walk she met a neighbor who asked her if she walked dogs for a living. "No, of course not," said Mary. "I am a nurse. I'm on leave right now because I had a nervous break-down."

"Well," said the neighbor. "I work all day and my cocker spaniel gets very lonesome. Would you mind walking her just for a while until you go back to work?" And that is how Mary became a professional dog walker. Her anxiety attacks stopped; her mar-riage blossomed; her happiness increased tenfold. She has at least ten canine "clients" now that she nurtures, and she cannot believe how happy she is. Nursing was her profession, but dog walking is her passion. She cannot imagine doing anything else.

If you look around, you will discover hundreds of Mary's and George's. There are people in your neighborhood and in your life who have dared to take a chance and try something unimag-inable. Some of them pursued a dream for a month or a year and then returned to the life they had been leading, but many of them discovered that very special thing that did more than put food on the table. They found the spirit that moved them one step closer to heaven.

I found my passion when I was seventy years old. I stumbled on a comedy college and decided to write a story about it. I had never seen stand-up comedy. I had never been in a bar or a comedy club. I did not know that comedy was a career. Writing

JAKARTA

that story opened up the world of comedy and entertainment for me and sent me on a journey that has lasted fifteen years. Never in all the careers I've pursued did it dawn on me that I was a performer. I discovered it purely by chance, just as you, too, can discover your passion if you dare to let your imagination wander. If you can be brave enough to take a first step that leads to something unexpected, you too may find your true destiny. There will be many side journeys, and all of them will be wonderful. All of them will add to the mix that you are becoming. And eventually you may settle on the thing you were always meant to do and be.

STOCKHOLM

CHAPTER 3

Recognize Golden Moments of Opportunity

Opportunity is missed because it is dressed in overalls and looks like work.
ANONYMOUS

We ought to pay attention to surprises, imaginations, fantasies, dreams, past loves, and chance encounters. Along the way, we can make our own rules. The first sixty-five years of life are tied to time schedules: we wake at eight in the morning, breakfast at eight-thirty, leave for work. Five o'clock, time to go home, battle rush-hour traffic, arrive home by six-thirty, dinner at seven, evening activity at eight, eleven o'clock to bed. And then we begin the whole rigmarole over the next day. For those who stay at home to care for families, the schedule is even more confining: up at six, prepare lunches for the children and breakfast for the family, see everyone off to wherever at eight, clean the kitchen, do the chores, prepare lunch, do afternoon activity (club meetings, volunteer work, errands), home by three, supervise children or drive them to their activities, prepare dinner at six, help children finish homework, prepare them for bed, join partner for the evening activity, clean up messes made by family. At midnight, collapse.

As the years go by, these routines change, but they never stop. We live our life with one eye on the clock and the other on the calendar of events and appointments that structure each day. Before we know it, we are well past middle age and have never found a moment to change direction. We have not thought about our potential; the truth is, we haven't had time to notice that we have one. We have been locked into an automatic, knee-jerk existence, and we never realized it didn't have to be that way. Take a moment to look back: there were clues all along the way, but you were in traffic, on your way to class, late for dinner, visiting your sister—and whoosh, that sparkling glimmer of something wonderful is gone.

When I was in college, I loved being part of our sorority entertainments. I sang about being a teapot. I acted in skits about underwear and other nonsense. I was in heaven on that stage. But I had a degree to earn, a vocation to create, a life to build, and singing nonsense to amuse a bunch of strangers was not on my bucket list. So I ignored the happiness I got from foolish moments of applause; I gave no importance to those theatrical thrills because I was too busy studying for finals, learning how to behave for a future husband I never found, grooming myself for ever more restrictive routines—and always, always watching the clock. Oh my God, it was time to study, time to eat, time to meet this one, time to help that one. How could there possibly be time to sing a silly song or become someone else in a play? Had I heeded those wonderfully fulfilling moments when I was nineteen and twenty, I would have begun the career I have today. I would have studied the art of acting and cabaret, indulged my love of performance art, and become a professional far sooner than I did. Theater was never considered a possibility. I was too busy being the "proper" person I was told to be.

And what about the people we marry? We date a variety of candidates, always considering if the two of us together will be greater than we are alone. We consider our mutual goals, the sharing of lifestyles, the possibility of working together to build the kind of life we've read about in magazines. So we settle on the one who is our most probable match, the person who shares our values and promises to give us the kind of life we saw our parents live.

But we will do it differently. We will do it our way. When we look back on our choices thirty or forty years later, we realize we've lived the very lives our parents lived. Oh, maybe some of the frills were different, maybe the projects were our own, but the basic routine—the work, the children, the house, the mortgage, the retirement—all that was exactly what our parents had shown us and expected of us.

I will never forget my Aunt Edith. If I had paid attention to her, my life's path would have veered sharply from the conformity I believed in. Aunt Edith saw her mother die in a charity hospital when she was ten years old. She and my mother climbed up the fire escape of that hospital to hold her mother's hand and say goodbye to her, because children were not allowed there. Aunt Edith gave not a whit for regulations. "I make my own rules," she told my shocked mother. Words from a ten-year-old. (This was in 1920–don't believe that it was only recently that rebels created unique lives for themselves.)

My aunt was gorgeous. Every young man in high school wanted to marry her, but she knew she wanted the love she never got from her strict stepmother, her demanding father, and the poverty that squelched her every dream before they took root. "You can marry a rich man and live the life we see in movies," my mother told her. "That's what I want to do."

But Edith didn't even hear her, because she had just met Sam. Sam was homely, awkward, and sweet as sugar. She adored him. When she met him he had nothing, not even a decent college degree, but she didn't care. Gorgeous Edith and fat, bumbling Sam; some would think at first sight he was so stupid because he flunked two years of school. They were a couple that people laughed at. How could that beautiful diamond of a girl stand him?

My aunt saw something wonderful in her suitor: Sam was kind, loving, and generous. Those were qualities she had never experienced, and she knew they were the real gold in life. Oh, she knew she could marry a rich, handsome man who would give her the trappings of a good life, yet she realized that none of those things mattered if there was no kindness, no love, and no caring. She married my Uncle Sam.

As their life unfolded, Sam became immensely wealthy and Edith took up golf, studied the piano, learned languages, and traveled the world with her portly lover. I was visiting my cousin one night when I saw my aunt getting dinner ready for Sam as he came home from work. The table was set for a banquet with flowers and with candles to light the meal. My aunt wore an evening dress and waited at the door to greet her husband when he entered the house. You could see that she couldn't wait to kiss him hello. When she took his hand and served him his cocktail he glowed, and I saw how satisfying marriage could be.

I had never seen my mother's eyes light up when Daddy came

Ridiculously Old and Getting Better

BROOKLYN

home. I never saw that kind of romance when I visited my friends' homes, or when I experienced my own marriage a few years later. My aunt and uncle were in their fifties and madly in love, because my aunt was smart enough to see that the right one for her didn't have to have a wonderful face or a hefty income. He wasn't smart or sophisticated. He was exactly what she needed, and exactly the kind of guy most of us would have passed by.

The golden moment happens and we let it slip by because we have to be somewhere in ten minutes. The magic unfolds and we ignore it because we are meeting our friend for coffee and cannot be late. The truth is, the happy human being, at any age, is the one clever enough to recognize those exquisite revelations and then act on them.

I read John Steinbeck's *Travels with Charley* when I was forty-eight and defeated by the life I thought I wanted. In that book, Steinbeck tells of his travels with his poodle across the country, relating stories about the interesting people he met along the way. I read that book and I knew what I needed to do. I didn't stop to think. I never considered the dangers, the foolishness of a forty-eight-year-old woman traveling alone through the southwest, and with a lot more than a poodle: I had two cats, two dogs, and a dream. And that dream turned out to be my personal gold ring. I spent a year and a half in a trailer and a truck, discovering not just America, but myself. I was lucky enough to recognize the golden moment, to see for one shimmering second the opportunities it might bring.

Life is such a busy affair. We think we have so much to do. Yet most of our obligations are in our head. They are no more real than our fears of failure, of being judged, and of falling short. They are dark, smothering mists that keep us lost in thankless routines. One day, if we are to emerge, we must push away the gloom that clouds our vision and stops our imagination from soaring to the skies. One day, if we are brave enough, we must grab that foolish idea, sing that song, paint that picture, fly off to a new country. Every one of us can do these things—but first we have to imagine them. First we need to take the time to realize that they are there for the having.

BERLIN

CHAPTER 4

What Are the Labels That Limit Who You Can Be?

Preconceived notions are the locks on the door to wisdom.
MARY BROWN

Mass media has created a universal picture of the good life. Each generation has created its own list of required components for being human, and we force ourselves into that accepted pattern no matter how uncomfortable it feels. What's more, we label ourselves and then stick to those labels despite what our heart tries to tell us.

Heterosexual, homosexual, Black, Caucasian, Asian, rich, poor, old, young: all these terms are labels for some aspect of our identity, but can also put fences around our existence. If you are a gay man, you love musical comedy, you like to decorate houses, and you mince instead of walk. If you are a lesbian, you wear masculine clothes, repair things, and hate men. That is ridiculous. Each human being is a unique mix of characteristics. Our inner logic tells us this. But as we listen to comedians, watch sitcoms, or read popular magazines, we see how these stereotypes are ingrained in our image of the homosexual life, the life of the young, the elderly, and each one of us.

Marcy married when she was twenty, and she had two children.

The days melted into weeks, months, and years and she knew she was fundamentally unhappy. She was a good and careful mother, but the whole marriage thing didn't fit who she wanted to be. She lived with her dissatisfaction until the children were in school. She knew she could not tolerate marriage, even though she liked and respected the man she lived with, she liked keeping house, and she enjoyed dressing in the latest fashions in *Vogue*.

This was in the 1960s, when homosexuality was considered a mental disease. Marcy knew she didn't want sex with men; she knew she was attracted to women. She also knew she loved being a mother. Because this was an era when the person she knew herself to be was not accepted, she lived alone with her children. She never told them the anguish she suffered from trying to fit into the framework of the "magazine image" of a wife and mother. And she was afraid her children would suffer because their mom was a misfit. She tried to hide her unhappiness but it often burst from her in erratic temper tantrums or angry, illogical behavior she could not control.

If you saw Marcy walking down the street, you would not look at her twice. She was just like every woman you might see on that street, wearing jeans and a shirt during the day, high heels and lipstick at night. She played cards with the girls, went to movies, and liked polishing her nails. She was an individual, just like everyone else in the world. I long for the day when everyone in this world can love who they love and marry who they love. Thankfully, this is true for many more than in Marcy's time, but by no means for all.

Marcy was unique because she was Marcy. Nobody fits into a

Ridiculously Old and Getting Better

label. Yet if we try to push ourselves to be what we feel is the acceptable pattern, everyone loses.

Think of the loss to society because Marcy was afraid to be herself. Her children saw and felt her unhappiness. They lived through their parent's marriage break up, the real situation hidden from them. In a society where Marcy can be with who she loves regardless of gender identity or sexual preference, she is a model for her children to create their own journey and become the people they truly want to be.

Stereotypes create a pattern of living, and if you follow them they give you the security of knowing you are dong all the "right" things. Rose was a devoted mother to her two sons, and when they married she adopted their wives as if they were her own. Today she takes her grandchildren to catechism, and on Sundays after church she cooks a huge meal for her whole family so they can spend the day and evening together. Everyone sits around a huge table and chatters to one another about everything from artificial food coloring to a landing on Mars. Rose's mother did that every Sunday for her and her sisters, and Rose does the same for her sons' families.

Now that Rose has retired from her job, she has even more time to be a good mom and grandma. She meets two of the grandchildren every day after class to help them with their homework. She has no time for herself because she takes care of the little boys after school Monday through Friday. Her husband would like the two of them to travel, to explore parts of the world they have never seen, but Rose swears she is happy doing just what she is doing: caring for her sons and their families.

Rose says she is happy caring for her grandchildren, however I can't help but notice that she seems to be living out the pattern she was brought up to follow. Could it be that she thinks this is her only option? Maybe her sons' families could occasionally live without dinner at her house or her chauffeuring services?

I ask Rose if she ever dreams about exploring the world, taking up a new hobby, or engaging in meaningful volunteer work outside of her immediate family. She says that all sounds lovely, but she feels that she needs to prioritize her children and grandchildren.

Whenever we break out of the expected pattern, there is an emotional and psychological price to pay. Robert knew from the time he was five that he was in the wrong body. He fought with his feelings and forced himself to live the life his parents told him a boy should want. He went to military school (and hated it), graduated, got a good-paying job, and married Diane. They had two lovely girls and bought a house in the suburbs. Finally, Robert could bear his life and his unhappiness no longer. He told Diane he couldn't endure being a man. That was not who he was. He saved his money and at great cost and physical pain underwent a sex change.

His two daughters still remember their daddy leaving the house one day and returning six months later as another mommy. Diane refused to leave the person she loved just because "he" became a "she." Robert was the father of her two daughters. It was this person she cared about. They live together now as Diane and Roberta.

So much unhappiness is caused by people examining their lives

Ridiculously Old and Getting Better

and saying to themselves, "This isn't what the TV programs and the magazines say is the way I should live and be happy." If each of us had the courage to say, "I am not a stereotype; I cannot conform to a rigid pattern someone else has decided is the good life," what a richer society we would have. There would be no dissatisfaction because Joe wasn't into football and beer or Susan liked to wrestle and box. We could allow everyone to create their own journey through life and meanwhile have the courage to live our own way. This acceptance is still in the future for our society. But each of us can look at our own lives now and say, "I must do it my way, because this is the way I function the best." Indeed the road to personal fulfillment is one that guides us to design our lives for ourselves, free of labels and stereotypes. Our life is our responsibility because it is the one thing that belongs to us. Each of us has the duty to make it sing.

BARCELONA

CHAPTER 5

What Does Our Existence Do for Humanity?

Every man bears the whole stamp of the human condition.

MICHEL DE MONTAIGNE

How many of us realize that our very existence is vital to the social mix we live in? Every human adds our own flavor to the whole, and his very presence improves life for everyone. In the rush of cramming activities into our day, we forget our own value and only think of what we must do to accomplish what we think is vital for today or will support our future plans. How few of us stop for a moment to think about who we really are and where we really want to go in life and honor our own intentions. Almost none of us learn to truly love ourselves. My friend Catherine told me that her new resolution was to never speak cruelly or condescendingly to herself; when she said that, I suddenly realized how abusive I am to myself. I could hear the many times I've told myself I am stupid or unlucky or destined to fail. I would never, ever talk to anyone else as cruelly as I chastise myself.

It can take years to learn to love yourself and accept who you are. When we were children we based our self-image on the opinions of our parents and our peers. It never occurred to us that we are the best judge of our own value. A low grade on a test, a punishment for a rule broken, an e-mail ignored—any one of these things can thrust us into a deep depression, which is not only unnecessary but invalid. Until we are in our fifties, or later, our life is jammed with imagined duties that will create the basis for the second half of our life, or so we think. If we lose our job, if the bread won't rise, the plumbing leaks, or we fall off a bicycle, we feel responsible for the failure.

We feel defeated because we expected the results to impress someone else. In mid-life and often beyond, we want and look for another's approval in almost everything we do, don't we? How sad that is! Because the most important approval and validation we need is our own. For years I believed that I had failed as a woman and as a member of society because I had not been successful at marriage and never had children. I ignored the eleven books I had written, the thousands of articles I had published, the hundreds of students I inspired. All of that didn't count, because my family and my peers didn't think those things mattered. They would ask me, "When will you get married?" or, "Don't you miss not having a baby?" I would suddenly be overwhelmed with my own lack of achievement. Now that I am older and look back on the path my life has taken, I realize that the degrees I earned, the travels I took, and the people whose lives I touched gave me a surfeit of pleasure and challenge, far more than I needed to live a delightful, rich life, then or now. Indeed, I would never trade this path for another.

It was not always so. One day when I was in my seventies, the penny dropped; I said to myself, "There must be a reason you are doing so many things you love to do and yet you are so unhappy doing them." I realized then that my unhappiness and feelings of inadequacy were caused by what I believed others thought about me. Yet, really, who knows you better than you do? The answer is no one, and no one is as interested in you as you are. You know your motives, you know the dreams you are working to make real. No one else is living your life.

The truth is that every day we grow just a little; we aren't the same person we were yesterday. We learn something, we forget something else; we try a new attitude, we consider a new thought—and we are that person until we begin the next day. We are the best person we can be at any given moment. And we are becoming different people who are better and better. If someone objects to us, it is his own insecurity pushing its way into the open. If someone criticizes you, it is her problem, isn't it? What have you done to hurt this person other than to be yourself? If someone sees your actions as politically incorrect, that is his opinion. Personality assessments are always in the eye of the beholder; they are never facts.

The trick is to value your difference. That unique something that is yours alone is the very contribution the world needs. When one of my students would cheat on an exam, I would say: "I don't want you to be like the person to the left or right of you. We already have one of them. Be you, the one who cannot answer that question but who can do something else better than they can. That is what we need from you."

We think of ourselves as small and inconsequential in the bigger picture. We think we do not matter and that the things we do have no impact on society. We are very, very wrong. When Barack Obama became president of the United States, many Black

YOKOHAMA

people throughout the world felt empowered. When Rosa Parks refused to sit in the back of the bus, she made a chip in racism that caused laws to be made and children of all races to go to school together.

Two little girls were selling lemonade at a stand they had set up in my hometown. When I saw it, I wrote a story about them for the local newspaper, and they became celebrities in their school. That small story made them feel important and confident enough to pursue other dreams and take other chances. We do not have to do anything that makes headlines to improve the world. We just have to make the effort to do what we think needs to be done.

DUBLIN

CHAPTER 6

Always Say Yes to Life

> The oldest, shortest words
> — yes and no — are those which
> require the most thought.
> PYTHAGORAS

All our life we are told what not to do. Don't do this; don't say that; don't wear this; don't think that. And we listen and obey because the people saying no are our parents, our peers, and the media, molding us into what they've determined is an acceptable image. Yet the only way we can discover who we really are is by experimenting with new ideas, trying unexpected things, and testing the limits life tries to create for us. The first step to happiness is learning to say yes.

Joanne had two little boys whom she adored, and a husband who was often drunk and out of touch with life. Her mother told her that if she divorced this man her boys would suffer terribly, because not only would they lose a father, they would lose the income he brought in. Joanne thought about what her life had been like living with this man for six years and she realized that it had been a prison of negativity. Every day she told the boys, "No, you can't do this, we can't afford it," or "No, you can't play here, you'll disturb your father," or "No, we can't go to a movie, your father took the car."

Her interaction with her husband was just as negative. "No, I am not going to that bar with you," and "No, I will not tell your boss you are sick. You have a hangover," and "No, you can't drive the car. You are drunk." The worst revelation was how negative she was with herself: "No, you can't make your life any better. You are stuck in this relationship. You will damage the boys emotionally. You can't bring up those children alone. You have no training to get a job."

Joanne began to look at her unhappy sons saddled with rules they didn't understand because of circumstances they didn't cause. She looked at herself, smudged with worries she saw no way to erase. She was wrapped in a blanket of unhappiness that tightened around her every day. One day, while she was fighting back her daily tears of frustration and anger, she came across Walt Kelly's *Pogo* comic: "We have met the enemy and he is us."

It was a life-changing moment. "That is the root of the whole problem," she told herself. "I am the enemy, not my husband, not my marriage, not my situation. If I stop saying 'I cannot do this or that' and start saying 'yes I can' to everything I want in life, it will all happen." And that is what she did. It wasn't easy and her life didn't change overnight, but her sombre cloud of unhappiness gradually lightened as she made positive plans to make things better for her boys and for herself. She divorced her husband and took nothing from him. "It took two of us to make this relationship and two of us to destroy it," she said. "We are both responsible for its failure. I am taking charge of my life now and I am taking responsibility for my decisions."

Ridiculously Old and Getting Better

She moved in with her mother and began to create a life that said "yes" to everything, bit by careful bit. She got a job with Avis Rent-A-Car, picking up cars at night and driving them back to their home office. She got another job with a Safeway supermarket tending greeting-card displays every morning. She was home by seven a.m. in time to get Michael, her six-year-old, ready for school and to send him off with his lunch pail and a kiss. She dressed Jimmy, her two-year old, and took him with her to the Safeway stores to tidy up and replenish their card displays. "I did not want to send him to day care," she said. "He was so little he couldn't explain what might bother him. He was quiet and shy and easily overlooked. And I did not want him to suffer by putting him in a cold, impersonal environment ."

She and her little one were home by three o'clock. Michael's school bus dropped him off at three-thirty and Joanne had his snack and a glass of milk ready for him. She and Jimmy listened to his tales of what he did in school. Then Joanne sent both children outside to play in the yard while she napped and their grandmother, Terry, watched them. Joanne woke up in time to help her mother prepare dinner for the four of them and tuck the boys in bed before she left to pick up an Avis car.

Not long after Michael had adjusted to his first-grade responsibilities, he came home and announced, "I want to be a Cub Scout." Terry shook her head. "You can't afford the fees and you can't afford the uniform," she told her daughter. "Tell him he will have to wait until you are earning a better salary." Joanne remembered *Pogo*, and she said, "He wants to be a Cub Scout. I will find a way to make that happen."

She called the Cub Scout leader and arranged for him to waive the cost of the manual each member needed and to find Michael a used uniform she could alter to fit him. In return she volunteered her services after school to help him with the troop. "When will you sleep?" asked Terry.

"It's only once a week," said Joanne. "I will catch up on Saturday." That first summer Joanne found a dilapidated Volkswagen bus, which she bought for one hundred dollars. She talked a friend into helping her make it drivable and safe. Taking a three-month leave of absence from her two jobs during Michael's school vacation, she and the two boys went off on a trip exploring the California coast. "It was a wonderful time for us," she said.

"We explored the forests and parks and walked around the tiny towns together. We hardly spent any money because we never went anywhere that charged admission. At night, I read them stories and we cooked out as much as possible. It was so much fun for us. The boys would help build the fire and do some of the cooking and everything tasted twice as good because we had made it together. I knew the minute we started out that this was going to become our family tradition. I wanted my sons to understand that the three of us could make a successful life because we had each other."

The years passed. Joanne got promotions in both jobs and her salary increased. The boys flourished, and soon it was time for Jimmy to enter the first grade. As soon as he was six, he announced that he wanted to be a Cub Scout just like his brother. "I called the school to see if there was a troop he could join

Ridiculously Old and Getting Better

and there wasn't one that year for the first grade," said Joanne. "Jimmy had been trying on Michael's old uniform for months in preparation for becoming a Cub Scout and I simply could not tell him he could not realize his dream. I knew what I had to do." Joanne became a scout leader, and Jimmy was the only member of her troop.

This was several years ago. Now both boys are full-fledged Eagle Scouts, and Joanne has been able to take a daytime job because they are both in school full-time. She is always home at three when they return from school, and she insists on taking time off every summer for the family trip. Every year life gets easier for them all. There is still very little money, but when her boys want a new adventure Joanne always finds a way to let them try it. "After all, we really have nothing to lose, do we?" she said. "No matter what happens, we always have each other. Nothing can take that away from us."

We may *want* to be positive about our life, but it is very difficult when the world is telling us that the worst will happen. "What if this goes wrong?" Perhaps in daring to recognize and act upon the opportunities life gives us, we gain hidden strengths to meet challenges.

Ellen woke up one morning and couldn't move. She thought she had pulled a muscle, but when she went to the doctor she discovered she had a severe case of multiple sclerosis. It had crept up on her suddenly and was particularly virulent. The doctor told her she would be unable to walk within months. Ellen was not the kind of person who accepted bad news. She believed that Lady Luck was always on her side. She had won the lottery not long before and was able to buy her family a house with that money. She had managed to kick a drug habit with determined effort. Her willpower alone had kept her clean for six years. If she could do those things, she could lick this horrible disease. However, despite her belief that she would never become physically immobilized, her muscle tone deteriorated; she went from crutches to a wheelchair even as she fought the illness with every medication and therapy her doctor prescribed.

Then something happened. Her husband, Joe, was at a business conference and was telling one of the other participants Ellen's sad story and about her hopeless diagnosis. "But my wife had the same thing!" said the man. "And now she is perfectly fine, because she had a stem cell replacement." Joe took down the name of the doctor, the hospital, and the specifics of the treatment and called Ellen. "You are going to walk again," he told her.

The treatment Ellen undertook was a new one and still experimental. She didn't know if it would cure her or kill her, but she took the chance. Because the treatment had not been approved by the Food and Drug Administration, it was not covered by any insurance. Lady Luck was on her side: she had enough money left from her lottery winnings to pay for the procedure. The process took several months, and while she was in the hospital recovering from the chemotherapy and radiation that removed her old cells and gave her new healthy ones, Ellen listened to comedy tapes. "They kill you to bring you back to life with stem cell replacement," she said. "I was determined to survive the treatments no matter how horrible they were, and I was convinced that laughter was the best antidote I could possibly take for the pain, the fear, and the depression that comes with them."

Ellen did survive the treatments. She had to battle side effects for years after, but while she was overcoming one setback after the other she managed to write a book about her experience and teach herself stand-up comedy. Today she is walking and although she still has a few problems with her eyes and her voice, she is comparatively healthy and always looking for new ways to enrich her life. If she had listened to all the medical experts, friends, and family who said, "No, do not take a chance on this untested cure," Ellen would be in a wheelchair today—or worse, she would not be here at all. She chose to say yes to an opportunity, and she is much the better for it.

Saying yes does not always bring positive results. Often that "yes" is only the beginning of a journey. The trick is to have the courage to try. Many of us will not embark on a new track in our lives because we are afraid of failure. Yet if we consider every experience to be a building block that is creating the structure of what we are becoming, we will be fortified to take a chance on the unknown.

I will never forget the time one of my students called me up and said, "Will I ever find the answer?" I was puzzled. After all, this call came with no preamble, no explanation. "The answer to what?" I asked. "To what life is about?" she said.

"Of course you will," I said. "When you die."

It takes a lifetime to become who you are. Only you can mold that life into something beautiful and exciting. No one can do that for you. Dying is not a tragedy; it is only an ending. The real loss is not daring to live while you are alive.

NEW YORK

CHAPTER 7

Love in the Autumn of Your Life

Pure love is a willingness to give without a thought of receiving anything in return.

PEACE PILGRIM

If there is one thing everyone wants, young or old, rich or poor, it is love. That exquisite connection with another human being validates us. It sharpens our senses so that an ordinary day becomes an unforgettable experience. It renews our energy and it makes our lives sing. When we were young, being "in love" meant sex, but when we are older, loving is not just a physical thing; it embodies all of who we are and can become. It is so much easier to love completely when we are over sixty. Mature love can be a beautiful thread that adds a shimmer to our life. We no longer tie our ability to love to physical desire. Instead, it is an overwhelming sensation that gives us wings. And the best part is, when we are older we can love with all our heart without the worry of being loved back.

Often it is in the most unexpected situations that we most easily recognize the signs that we are loved. I am very short. I do interviews at my local television station, and when I sit across from a typically-sized person, I look like an ant interviewing a giant. Our station has an engineer who is two years older than I. I loved him from the moment I met him. Dan is a recovered alcoholic;

he is very quiet and reserved, yet he emanates kindness. His wife died about ten years ago and he decided that he had to turn the page on his old life and create something new for himself. And so although he had been in construction and professional gardening, he decided to become an apprentice engineer at the station.

Dan was different from the others trying to learn the ropes at our station, because he was always so considerate of all of us who were novices at performing in front of a camera. Whenever I saw him, I was flooded with happiness. I knew he would never hurt my feelings or diminish me in any way. His very presence made me feel important.

The two of us never spent any time together, but I knew that he respected me and wanted to help me create an interesting, dynamic program. One day all the camera people were laughing at how tiny I looked when I talked with my guests. I have to say, their banter made me feel very inadequate. After all, I am the star of the show and I didn't like the idea that I looked ludicrous when I spoke to my guests.

Dan said nothing and of course he did not join in with the teasing. He would never do that kind of thing. The next week I came to the station to do another program, and when I looked at our show set, I saw a pillow on the chair I sat in. I knew immediately how it got there. Dan had thought of a way to make me look taller, and he did something about it. I knew then that he loved me in a very beautiful way.

And I love Dan back. The two of us know how we feel about each other even though we have never discussed it. We wouldn't dream of sharing a bed or sitting across the breakfast table from one another. We have both done that kind of thing and are not about to do it again. Yet we are in love. I can feel our affection whenever we are in the same room. It is thick as a down comforter and it always warms my heart.

I met Sarah when I was performing at a show. I arrived late because I could not find a parking place. She was taking tickets at the door and when she heard of my dilemma, she took my car keys from me and parked my car while I got ready for my performance. Some time later when I broke my foot, I could not cook for myself because I would lose my balance if I stood on one leg to chop vegetables or prepare a casserole. Most of the entertainment community knew I had hurt myself, but I never thought of contacting them for help. We weren't friends even though we were friendly with one another. Two days after I arrived home from the hospital, Sarah walked into my kitchen ladened with groceries and started cooking. "I thought you might need some help," she said.

Sarah never asked if I needed her, and I never asked her for help. Yet she returned three times a week and made meals for me that I could put in the microwave. Those meals were delicious. "You are such a great cook, you should open a restaurant," I said, but she shook her head. "I only cook for people I care about," she said. Sarah and I had met and bonded months before, but we never chatted on the telephone or met for lunch. I barely knew her until she came to my house to cook and share ideas with me. My well-being meant enough to her to cross a bridge and drive the forty-five minutes to my home to be certain I was fed. That is the purest kind of love anyone can receive. I cannot think of any act more beautiful to me than watching Sarah cook and tell me about

SINGAPORE

her dreams while she stood at my stove.

The older you are, the easier it is to realize *agape*, a love for all humankind that has its own kind of passion. The beauty of *agape* is that it costs nothing and demands nothing. The other person's presence is what makes you happy. I had always thought of love as a connection between a man and a woman. I never gave much thought to developing the ability to love for the sake of loving alone.

My friend Pam is an expert at that kind of love. She belongs to a young mothers' group with her tiny daughter Heather. One day she picked up the newspaper and, to her horror, read that one of the mothers in her group had been run over by a tractor and killed. Pam did not know this woman's husband; in fact, she had rarely spoken to the woman herself. Still, she knew how important it was for everyone in the group to mobilize their efforts to help this man take care of his six-month-old daughter. Pam created a schedule and asked the other members of the group to help her aid the young man and his child. Each woman took a day of the week to provide food and care for the infant while the husband was at work.

Pam did not ponder her decision to run this project. She didn't ask her husband if he would mind caring for Heather while she went to the other child's home to make sure there was a meal for the widower and proper formula for the child. Her heart was filled with love for others, not just for her husband and child. When she saw a need, she expressed that love abundantly. Today Pam shows her love when she runs marathons to raise funds for cancer research. She has reached out to help me find a good home. She does all this because she loves humankind. And her very act of loving gives love back to her.

It is this kind of love that older people can give more easily, often because our family obligations have diminished and we can give our time to others without someone else paying the price of neglect or inattention. The time we give to others does not deprive our children of our presence or our boss of a day's work. As elders we are free to use our time to enrich ourselves by giving to others.

This is not to say that older people are past romance. No, indeed. We too can thirst for romantic love, and that love, when it happens, can be more satisfying than the lust we felt in our younger years. It is a love of the whole person without thought to what he can give, or to the appeal of her sexual performance. When we are older, we can love someone of any age and every human being we meet. The best part is that we receive the joy we give. That kind of love energizes us and makes us want to do more with our life than we ever thought of doing alone.

Brenda is in her sixties. She was an aspiring biographer who suffered from chronic fatigue syndrome. Always too exhausted to work an eight-hour day, she decided to establish herself as a writing teacher. But try as she did, she never could get a class established and she was always on the brink of poverty. She lived from job to job, and those opportunities became fewer every year. Then she met Brian. Brian is in his late seventies and he is a prince of a man. The two of them are spending more and more time together, and as the months go by, Brenda seems to be gaining initiative and energy. There is a lift to her step; her eyes are bright and interested in the world around her. She no longer feels so alone. Even better, she has begun to have more success creating her classes. She is beginning to enjoy financial success as well. Love creates happiness and happiness fosters success. They seem to go together.

Indeed, as elders we fall in love with the same passion, the same longing to be with the loved one, the same worry that the love will not be returned. Yet sometimes the love we feel is not expressed back to us in the way we would like. It may feel like it is not returned at all. But it is there, and if we are wise we will recognize it and return it in our own way. And somehow the very act of loving someone becomes enough.

I adore David. He is forty years my junior and lives in another country. He has a beautiful wife, Sally, and three of the most wonderful children ever. David and I sometimes go out for dinner together to discuss the human condition. Even though we are generations apart, we see eye to eye on so many things that it is a joy to exchange ideas with him. He is my love and I am his. It has never occurred to either of us to consummate this love in any way other than across a dinner table. Yet we both know that if one of us were in trouble, the other would cross an ocean to help. That is the kind of love older people especially can give to the young. That is the kind of passion they can share. It is a love that makes no demands. It has nothing to prove. The only thing it cares about is that the loved one flowers in his own individual way. Love does not possess. Instead, it frees both to become more than they ever thought they could be.

COLOGNE

CHAPTER 8

Preconceived Notions Are Not Laws

Success is not final; failure is not fatal. It
is the courage to continue that counts.
WINSTON CHURCHILL

When we are children, our parents show us by example what "the good life" is all about. My mother and father lived in the same house and shared a bedroom. They had their own separate routines, and they followed them alongside one another. They never did anything together at home, except eat dinner. Sometimes, on a weekend, they would go out together to visit a relative or indulge in a movie. My mother would dress in something lovely that made her look like a stranger. She doused herself in Chanel No. 5 and my father would hold her coat for her, take her arm, and they would leave. They left me with Nettie.

I loved Nettie. She never told me what to do or how to do it. She just loved me for who I was. Nettie was Black and walked on crutches. My mother made it very clear to me: "Nettie is poor, crippled and disadvantaged. We are being kind to her by allowing her to work in our nice house. She lives in a horrid place with other Black people who have no money."

The message was that if I wanted a good life, I would not be like Nettie. She was a maid. She was not successful—everyone wanted success, didn't they? I had a hard time understanding that because I had no ideas about success. I just wanted to be with Nettie because she made me feel perfect. I thought Nettie was God. In fact, I was sure of it. Nettie loved me and told me so every time we were together. Whatever I did was wonderful and she was proud of me. If I scribbled two lines on a paper, she told me I would grow up to be an artist. "Is that good?" I asked. "That is the very best thing you can be," said Nettie. "Artists make the world beautiful." My parents did not seem to love anyone. They certainly did not love each other; in fact they didn't seem to even like each other. They weren't that fond of me. Mother fed and clothed me and told me what to do and what not to do. *Stand up straight. Go out and play. Be polite to your Aunt Beck. Don't talk to strangers. Wash your face. Tell the truth. Chew with your mouth closed. Go to your room.* She told me often what I was not and what I should be.

When Daddy was home he had similarly strict demands. *Be quiet. Don't bother me. Read a book. Go sit over there. Go to your room.* I always felt the tension and the suppressed anger between them. I was never very comfortable when we were all together because Daddy was reading the paper, Mother was doing dishes or talking on the telephone, and I was not allowed to say anything at all because it would upset them.

I thought that if I wanted to be happy, I needed to live a life like the one they were living. But in that life I saw in my home no one was happy; everyone ignored each other, and people didn't hug. It didn't make sense. I was taught that the worst thing that could happen to me was to end up like Nettie: poor and disabled. Never mind that Nettie was loving, affectionate, approving. My parents assured me that those things would not lead to my success. By the time I went to school, I understood the direction I must go if I wanted to be happy and successful; if I wanted approval from my parents and everyone else who lived like they did. And I didn't like that direction at all. It was uncomfortable for me.

At school I got a different picture of what happiness could be. I learned there are many kinds of success. I met children from other cultures, and they shared their vision of what happiness and success meant to them. Hidemi's dad was a professor at Stanford, and Juanita's father was a doorman at the Hillcrest Hotel. Richard's father was a doctor who made lots of money. Wanda's father abandoned her when she was three years old. Yet, all of us were being taught by teachers who shared my parents' vision of "the good life."

Children are not as stupid as adults think they are. It didn't take me long to figure out that Hidemi's definition of happiness included a lot of books and a bowl of rice for supper. Juanita preferred grits for breakfast and Wanda was lucky if she got anything at all. Richard had a nanny and never saw his parents, except sometimes at dinner on weekends. I personally thought Richard was very lucky. What I learned at school besides reading, writing, and arithmetic was that all three girls were fun to be with, and that Richard was boring. I also figured out that a dream is a very personal thing. Each of us has our own vision of "the good life." The interesting thing is that each person's description of that life is unique. I gradually evaluated and incorporated aspects of their visions into a picture of my own life journey. It no longer reflected the accepted social expectations.

For many, the first fifty years seem to be spent trying to conform to the lifestyle our parents lived. This may have been modified by the people we met in school or read about in magazines. Whenever we become friends with people who come from different backgrounds, a little of what they believe in rubs off on us. Still, even though we don't particularly want the lifestyle we saw in our homes, some part of us is brainwashed to think it is the only way to live.

By the time we are fifty, we have established an income level and standard of living; we know who we are. We are in a relationship or are we loners; we have identified our passions, mostly by knowing how much they differ from or resemble our parents'. We know if we prefer a baseball game to a night at the symphony, a vacation on the beach to one exploring the museums of Europe. Sadly, most of us have no idea what we want to be. We only know what we have been told we should be. But here's the good news. That mid-century mark is a very good time to search our psyche: "Okay, now I know who I am. It is time to go after what I really want to be."

Did you always love dancing? Then enroll in a dance class and compete in dance marathons. Did you love to sing? Join a choir. Had you always dreamed of doing an archaeological dig in Africa? Get on-line and find yourself a safari. Now is the time to break out of that stereotype people fed you about who were supposed to be. Those people do not rule you anymore. You do not have to obey your mom or your teacher. At fifty and beyond you don't have to worry about your boss, either. If he doesn't treat you with respect, you can walk out. You know your value.

Do you have the courage to break out of the stereotype that has imprisoned you? Are you willing to dare to become yourself? Give it a try for a day, a week, or a month. Meet a stranger for lunch. Go to a museum. Take swing dancing. Swim naked. And if the new career, the new hobby, the new vacation doesn't feel comfortable, try something else. My mother always wanted to sing opera, but she never tried to do it. I always wanted to hula hoop. I tried it. I could not do it. I took up piano instead.

You only have one life to live, and it is up to you to make it a good one. If you get out there and sing your song, it makes no difference if you are on key. After all, the woods would be very silent if the only birds who sang were the ones who sang best.

COLOGNE

CHAPTER 9

Let's Take Part in Our World

"No life is a waste," the Blue Man said.
"The only time we waste is the time we
spend thinking we're alone."
MITCH ALBOM

It is easy to lose sight of the big picture. When we reach a certain age, we may no longer worry about the quality of the schools in our town or the consistency of city services. We think we are past concerns about new construction or the promotion of art. We have our pension and we have established our way of life. Why worry if the police are being underpaid or there isn't enough housing for the poor. We are not in the police force; we have a place to live.

And so we vote against raising taxes to improve city services or finance help for the young and the needy in our society. We do not realize that our lack of support is actually diminishing the safety, care, and conveniences in our own life. What we forget is that the child we educate will be the one who understands the need for special care for the elderly. He will be the one who gets the ambulance to us on time, who charges us a reduced rate for entertainment and creature comforts.

When you vote in a civic election or pay taxes for city improvements, you are supporting a society that gave you the amenities you now enjoy. And you are preserving those amenities for others, including those who come after you. But we owe our society more than our votes and tax payments. When we no longer have to report for work each day, we can donate our time to improving opportunity for others, including ourselves. We do not need to give money; we can give of ourselves instead.

My friend Lily came to this country from Germany. She could not speak a word of English when she got here. She took advantage of free English classes, history classes, and courses to help her become a citizen. She joined special clubs for new Americans that were sponsored by the local YMCA, and she gradually became part of her town, her state, and her new country. Now she is in her late sixties and she devotes one day a week to tutoring children in reading and English. It is her way of paying back for the services she received to acclimate her to America. But she is doing far more than just repaying a debt. She is helping one individual at a time master the technique of living in society, learning the language, and understanding basic communication skills. She is also making a better world for her grandchildren by educating those with whom they will associate as they live and work in a society where we all can understand one another.

When I was young, I lived in Toledo, Ohio, a city with a band of parks going though it. In the 1970s the city council created a very special place called Crosby Park with a botanical garden, a garden for the blind, and a place where artists could display their work in a gala festival of the arts that was unmatched by any other festival in the city. It cost millions of taxpayer dollars, and there was a swell of resentment that so much money was

Ridiculously Old and Getting Better

not spent on police activities or repairing roads or financing the war on drugs.

My Aunt Sunne, who had been a farm girl, moved to Toledo. As she aged, each home she lived in took her farther and farther from the earth she loved to work. When she was in her seventies she lived in a high-rise apartment with no garden. There was nothing in the world she loved as much as having me drive her to Crosby Park, where she could identify the plants and flowers as we strolled along the winding paths. Each year I took her to the art exhibits; she loved talking to the artists and seeing how their work had progressed from one year to the next. The joy that park gave my aunt and the thousands of people who walked through it was worth millions of dollars to those people, because the park did so much to enhance their happiness and their pleasure.

This is what our society gives us and why at every age we must continue to contribute to its growth and to the services it offers all of us. As the Greek proverb goes, "A society grows great when old men plant trees whose shade they know they shall never sit in." That is what the good life is about. When we are asked to pay a tax on a service that does not apply to us, it is the debt we owe for all the services we do enjoy that make our lives more pleasant and easier to manage.

BANGKOK

CHAPTER 10

One Day

> A sane society . . . is not going to be ordained for us. We must make it ourselves.
>
> HELEN KELLER

Let us take one day and fill it with reason and compassion for one another. On that day, each of us will value everyone else's uniqueness, their individuality. We will not judge those we meet until we give ourselves the time to know and understand them. If we do not approve of another person, it is our problem. That person has the same right to exist and to strive for his own brand of happiness as we do.

After all, the richness in our world is counted by our differences. No human being can be a carbon copy of another, even if he were foolish enough to try. On this one day, we will allow everyone to have a variety of opinions; we are different people whose eyes see every event colored by our own experience. And that is a very good thing. We will listen carefully to each original idea and we will not be threatened by it because, really, it is only an idea; it isn't a law.

Every age in the life cycle will be given the respect it deserves. We will not diminish a child by telling her she is too young to understand why she cannot run into the street. Instead, we will take the time to explain the dangers to her and then have enough faith in her intelligence to allow her to make her own decisions. She is not stupid just because she has not lived as long as we have. We will not tell a teenager he does not know what love is, because if we search our memories we will remember that our first loves were our sweetest. It was only adult disparagement that soured those memorable but fleeting moments for us and made us doubt them. We will encourage those of us who are afraid to love completely for fear that love will not be returned. We will remind them that a beautiful moment is just that: a moment. It need not last forever. It is only a moment.

We will not disparage those among us who are physically or mentally different. We will understand that we are responsible for labeling a characteristic a disability. After all, everyone is who they are, no more and no less. Each one is part of the very mix that makes ours a rich and diverse society. Society is like a bowl of fruit or beautiful glass of wine: the more flavors, the more exciting it is.

On this day, we will not retaliate when someone snaps at us. We will understand that this person is reflecting his own pain even as he lashes out at us. We have all felt that same hurt. No one is expected to love everyone he meets. On this day, we will allow people to have the right to continue their journey on their own terms. On this day we will allow everyone the right to be angry as well as the right to determine his own fate. It is their individual destiny. On this day, the cost of things will not have anything to do with our appreciation of them. We will know that we do not have to own everything we admire, and we will realize how little is necessary for our well-being. It isn't an accumulation of

Ridiculously Old and Getting Better

things that creates a good life; it is our sense of belonging and the knowledge of our growth. We do not need that fancy car or expensive pair of shoes. Why bother with a diamond necklace or a cosmetic treatment that will enhance our external appearance? On this day, let's concentrate on feeding our hearts. This day we will love ourselves. We will allow ourselves to try new adventures, and if they don't end the way we thought they would, we will not chastise ourselves. We will rejoice because we added one more experience to the many we have had before, experiences that made our life richer and more exciting.

This day we will not regret anything we do, because we will know that we are doing our best. We will realize that we are as perfect as we can be today and the experiences we have today will make us a different, more exciting human being tomorrow.

We will know that we are beautiful. We are all stunning magazine covers— gorgeous each in our own way. We will not disparage a drooping jowl, an aging chin, or thinning hair. On this day we will realize that those wrinkles and that arched nose are all components of a unique individual. Who wants to be the mirror of another? How much better it is to be ourselves.

We will respect the world we live in on this day. It is our responsibility to create and preserve a lovely world. We will not deface roads and spaces with things we no longer want. We will take a moment to appreciate the grass growing at our feet and the flowers that dare to blossom in a world that so often deprives them of food and light. If we do not take time to feed our souls, we will be nothing but robots slogging through the same routine every day, and we will miss the burst of pleasure at a soft breeze or a single rose blooming along our path. But on this day we will see the beauty that is everywhere, and we will know that it is the food that makes us human. Today, we will know that nothing we do or think or say is an ending. It is instead a new beginning that we can fashion into something wonderful, not just for ourselves but for everyone around us. There is no such thing as failure. Everything we do, say, or think is part of the mix that propels us toward who we are becoming.

We will make this day a happy one. After all, unhappiness is a choice. Why should we opt for displeasure and tears when we can have satisfaction and joy? We have the power to label each experience we have as good or bad. When we tell ourselves the moment is ugly, it is, because we made that judgment. Perhaps, if we look at it through a different lens, it can appear as a lovely experience. We each have the power to transform any negative into a positive. It is all in how we see it. Remember, the world outside is not going to adapt to us; the only changes we can make are within ourselves.

This day, let us realize that our home is in our hearts. The door we open and the bed we sleep in have nothing to do with our sense of belonging and our peace of mind. We will give every-one we see space to be themselves and grow at their own rate, because it is to our advantage to allow everyone to live their own life in their own way.

We will allow ourselves to be outrageous. We will indulge in that piece of chocolate cake, or dare to ride a roller coaster. We will forget the schedule we planned and have a picnic. Maybe we will kiss a stranger. We will paint a picture or sing a song we have

Ridiculously Old and Getting Better

never heard before. We will step outside the box we have built for ourselves and taste the novelty of something different.

And at this day's end, we will not worry about what we did not do. That is a waste of energy. Perhaps some things are better left undone. Perhaps they are better accomplished tomorrow. All we need do at the end of this particular day is appreciate what it has brought to us and what we have learned from it to make a better tomorrow.

Let us try to do all these things for just one day. Who knows, it might very well lead to another, and before we know it we will have changed the world, one day at a time.

MANILA

Living the Good Life

There are three ingredients in the good life: Learning, earning and yearning.
CHRISTOPHER MORLEY

Ezekiel Emanuel was fifty-seven years old when he wrote the essay I will tell you about. He is a physician specializing in cancer and is vice provost and professor at the University of Pennsylvania. He is a very smart man. Last October he wrote an essay saying he wanted his life to end at seventy-five.

He is a fool.

When I was fifty-seven, I had no idea what fun I could have once I crossed the line and left the place where productivity, beauty, and fame topped the list of what I needed to make my day. When I was fifty-seven, I cared that my face was drooping, my hearing was getting dull, and my walk was slowing, step by step. Now at my age, I love my wrinkled face. It gets me every perk I could possibly want. I step into a packed car in the bus and at least three gorgeous men stand up so I can rest my wrinkled bum on a seat. I board a train and take a premium seat that is labeled "priority seating" just because I have been around a long time.

When I carry packages up or down stairs, there is always someone to carry those bundles for me, and usually with a smile. I hop on a bus (yes, I can still hop) and sit down without worrying about the fare. I go to movies, plays, and concerts and pay at least twenty-five percent less than everyone else including all those youngsters under sixty with low-paying jobs and expensive taste.

If I am in a queue and it is taking too long, I clutch my heart and gasp a little; that gets me to the head of the line before I can exhale. I stand at a counter rummaging though endless coins I cannot recognize without my glasses and not once has anyone said, "Hurry up, lady." No, indeed. Invariably there will be some kind soul who will hold my packages while I search for coins I dropped in the bottom of my purse, and the clerk will always smile and say, "Take your time, darling."

And that brings me to another point: everyone, men, women, and even children, address me as "darling," and they mean it. The very things I did at fifty that annoyed the hell out of everyone; the missteps and accidents I had in my twenties, which made two husbands leave me: all are absolutely adorable now that I am in my ninth decade.

But it isn't just the attitude of everyone around me that has made life so very sweet these days. It is my attitude. I am no longer concerned with what I see in the mirror. It never got me much when I was younger and I don't expect it to be the eighth aesthetic wonder of the world now. That means that all the time, money, and anguish I spent in beauty shops and on countless rejuvenation creams, skin enhancers, hair boosters—all of it is now spent on more rewarding activities, such as eating anything I want because, what the hell, by the time I am too obese for my coffin I won't care. I won't have to spend the extra money for a larger coffin either. Social services will.

I am at the age now where I can spend as much as I want for anything I want: if I run out, I can get benefits. My intention is to reduce my bank balance to zero and then apply for residence in a home. I am not worried about my liver either. It's held up this long, hasn't it?

When I was in my fifties I anguished because I had not made a visible mark in the world. No one knew who I was. My name never made a headline. Now I realize that it isn't the publicity you get for what you do; it is what you do that matters. If it makes me happy and I am involved, then hooray; not getting some award or a mention in someone's column won't change that. It took me this long to understand that.

Ezekiel Emanuel says, "But here is a simple truth that many of us seem to resist: living too long is also a loss. It renders many of us, if not disabled, then faltering and declining, a state that may not be worse than death but is nonetheless deprived. It robs us of our creativity and ability to contribute to work, society, the world."

And I say, "How does he know that? He hasn't gotten there yet." Well, I have, and I can honestly say that my walk is slower but I get where I want to go and I do not feel deprived. I enjoy my life just as it is. I do not have the same desires I had at twenty or thirty or forty because that is not the stage of life I am in right now. My perspective has improved. I know now that nothing is forever. The pain I feel will go away; the insult I felt will evaporate. I have confidence in myself. I trust my judgment for me. I don't want to go to bars and find a hot sexpot to take me to bed. That doesn't interest me anymore. I don't want to wear uncomfortable clothes that reveal my nether parts because my nether parts are

SAN FRANCISCO

not the focus of my pleasure anymore. My mind and my heart are the hungry organs now and I do everything I can to feed them. It is more fun and not as sloppy.

It took me a long time to understand that life is like a card game. You take the hand you get and play it the best you can. It does no good to bemoan what you didn't get or begrudge others for what they have achieved. You do not know what they had to do to get there. I am happy now with the life I have, but I am not content to stand still. Not yet. I still have big plans for my future.

I am living in the now. What is past is gone; I am not that person anymore. I don't look good in her clothes. I do not want to walk in her shoes—they would pinch my bunion. I do not want to waste the time she did on the telephone bemoaning what she didn't have. I love my current life and I am determined to make the most of it. I will not waste my energy worrying about what I will do when I am ninety, because I am not there yet. When I am, I have no doubt that I will have adjusted to the difference in my motor abilities, my memory, and my diminished lifestyle. I do not know how I will like it until it happens.

Do not get me wrong. I do not want to waste away in a hospital bed any more than you do. But I have reached an age where I am determined to let my body fall apart at its own pace. I do get my flu shots but I am not sure I would allow any procedures to prolong my life if I had a terminal illness.

I am not afraid of dying. It is after all the most dramatic event in our life other than birth. I cannot recall being afraid when I exited my mother's body and I have no intention of being consumed with fear about my death, because I have no idea when it will happen or how. When I am there, I will deal with it. Hopefully it will be a grand and dramatic departure.

My goal right now is to live abundantly. I will not spend one iota of the time I have in worry, because worry never accomplished anything and I have a lot I need to do. I want to learn to fan dance. I see myself shimmying and swaying to the music, showing off my cute bum and my shapely legs—and then turning to the audience, peeking out of the fans with a face that looks for all the world like an abandoned prune that needs ironing. It should have an amazing effect on the crowd.

I want to play the ukulele and tap dance while I do it. I want to explore the nooks and crannies of a Europe I have read about, and I want to make a lot of strangers laugh. I want to fall in love the right way this time—loving who he is, not how he looks, what he buys me, or what he wears. The size of his wallet or his dick are not barometers of love for me anymore. They never were, but I thought they were. I know better now. I cannot be bothered regretting the hump on my back or the arthritis that has gnarled my fingers. They still work, and while they do I am using them.

I have done the accepted thing: I have prepared a directive that tells everyone not to resuscitate me and not to use any artificial means to keep me alive. I have donated all the organs that work to anyone who needs them, although why anyone would want my ears is something I cannot fathom. My kidneys however are stellar and I hope the person who gets them appreciates how beautifully they work, as they have worked for me.

I do not want to lie in a hospital bed on life support with medical

Ridiculously Old and Getting Better

science keeping me alive, and I know very well that is a decision I must make while I have all my faculties and can prepare the proper papers to keep an exuberant medical staff from pumping up my lungs and stimulating a heart that no longer wants to beat. I have created that directive, but that is all I have done. I am ready and willing for death to happen when it is ready for me. My mother always said I arrived two months after I was due. "You were always slow," she said. "Right from the beginning."

But I got here, didn't I?

I hope my exit will be cleaner and faster, but if it isn't…well, I cannot know what it will be like until it happens. I am determined to only die once, and that will be on the day my heart stops beating and my lungs give me no air— not one minute before.

The trick is to live, to live as fully, as beautifully, and as daringly as you can. Reach for every star and don't be afraid to meet the price, do the work, and pay the dues to get you there. There is no dream that is impossible. Wallace Stegner says we do not die from a disease. We die because we are finished.

I am not finished. Are you?

> The longer I live,
> the more beautiful life becomes.
> FRANK LLOYD WRIGHT

REVIEWS AND SOUNDBITES FROM THE AUDIENCE

"I run The Athena Network southeast groups which are networking groups for women in business. I am always trying to find inspirational women speakers for my groups so I was absolutely delighted when I met Lynn.

Lynn has spoken in all of my groups and the ladies have found her amazingly inspirational. Each talk has been very different and tailored to the audience, and Lynn left the ladies laughing and feeling very energized. I would fully recommend Lynn to speak at any event. She has the ability to engage any audience. She is a wonderful lady and a blessing to be around."
~ *Michala Rutherford, The Athena Network, UK*

"I think it's very...amazing, to see a woman...this age, give me some, uh, vibrations."
~ *Lars from Sweden*

"I thoroughly enjoyed the show and I hope I have that much fun when I'm eighty-one!"
~ *Alice from Edinburgh, Scotland*

"Just seen the show up in Edinburgh, definitely the best show I've seen all festival, and I've seen a lot."
~ *Steve from Hartlepool, England*

"Incredible! I'm recommending to all my friends."
~ *Xanthia from Edinburgh, Scotland*

"I was NOT expecting the nappies."
~ *Di from Singapore*

"It made me cry, beautiful."
~ *Carol from Edinburgh, Scotland*

"Really, really, really, really great."
~ *Maxim from France*

"Fantastic! Go see it."
~ *Sarah from Florence, Italy*

"Really funny, I'm so glad we stumbled across it."
~ *Jane from Oxford, England*

"I had to see it again and I brought my husband, my friends, and my Mum."
~ *Margaret from Peterhead, Scotland*

"Absolutely brilliant."
~ *Eleanor from Stoke-on-Trent, England*

"Superbly first class. Uplifting, unique entertainment."
~ *Christopher from Surrey, England*

"It was a wee bit like an erection darlin'."
~ *Fergus from Glasgow, Scotland*

"Hilarious, I can't remember the last time I saw something as funny."
~ *Pauline from the Isle of Wight, England*

"The song at the end was utterly inspirational."
~ *Emma from Australia*

"What a sexy woman."
~ *Alex from Edinburgh, Scotland*

"The 'Where the Boys Are' song was my favorite: funny and sad."
~ *Thomas from Poland*

"This is the fourth time I've seen the show, it gets better every time! Love bringing my friends."
~ *Saskia from Edinburgh, Scotland*

"She is such a tart. I love her."
~ *Jemaime from Australia*

"Very, very funny. I loved when she gave me the condom. Wonderful singer."
~ *Pasi from Finland*

"If she ever gets into the cougar business—or 'saber-toothed tiger' as she says since she's past seventy—let her know I'm twenty-two and interested."
~ *Charlie from London, England*

CPSIA information can be obtained
at www.ICGtesting.com
Printed in the USA
BVHW090535150921
616750BV00012B/1168